W9-CQL-584

*To*_____

*From*_____

A Little Spoonful of
Chicken Soup for the Woman's Soul™

Published by Blessings Unlimited, Pentagon Towers
P.O. Box 398004, Edina, MN 55439

Photos by Barbara Peacock
Design by Lecy Design

ISBN 1-58375-549-7

The best and most beautiful things in the world cannot be seen or even touched. They must be felt with the heart.

Helen Keller

A friend may well be reckoned the masterpiece of nature.

Ralph Waldo Emerson

$\mathcal{L}$ove cures people—both the ones who give it and the ones who receive it.

~ *Karl Menninger*

*J*ust don't give up trying to do what you really want to do. Where there's love and inspiration, I don't think you can go wrong.

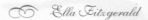 *Ella Fitzgerald*

$\mathcal{I}$ have become more of a feather myself as the years have flown by: I am less resistant to what life offers up, and the pressures flow over me much more easily.

Melody Arnett
CHICKEN SOUP FOR THE WOMAN'S SOUL

$\mathcal{M}$y wedding dress hangs in the back of my closet. I can still zip it up (as long as I'm not in it!).

Rebecca Christian
<small>CHICKEN SOUP FOR THE WOMAN'S SOUL</small>

$\mathcal{I}$ have let myself dream freely and pursue the dreams that really move me.

Chris Mullins
A SECOND CHICKEN SOUP
FOR THE WOMAN'S SOUL

"This is the day the Lord hath made.

Rejoice and be glad in it."

Maybe everything will be all right,

she thought.

Ann Seely
as submitted by Laura J. Teamer
CHICKEN SOUP FOR THE
WOMAN'S SOUL

$\mathcal{N}$o matter how abandoned and alone
we feel, somehow, somewhere, someone
knows and cares.

Mary L. Miller
Chicken Soup for the Woman's Soul

$\mathcal{H}$aving changed my focus to such positive thoughts, I couldn't believe the difference it made in my life. I felt like laughing again.

Laurie Waldron
CHICKEN SOUP FOR THE WOMAN'S SOUL

$\mathcal{G}$reat thoughts speak only to the thoughtful mind, but great actions speak to all mankind.

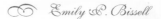 *Emily P. Bissell*

The love you share is the love
you keep.

Drue Duke
A SECOND CHICKEN SOUP
FOR THE WOMAN'S SOUL

$\mathcal{M}$ost people need to hear those "three little words." Once in a while, they hear them just in time.

◁ *Bobbie Lippman*
CHICKEN SOUP FOR THE WOMAN'S SOUL

$\mathcal{I}$ am grateful for the blessings in my life now, and I accept the events in my life as gifts of growth that create strength of character and strength of faith.

Joan Fountain with Carol Kline
CHICKEN SOUP FOR THE WOMAN'S SOUL

$\mathcal{W}$e don't see things as they are, we see them as we are.

 Anaïs Nin

She gave us the ability to see beauty even in the face of adversity.

Marsha Arons
CHICKEN SOUP FOR THE WOMAN'S SOUL

I always say yes first; then I ask, "Now, what do I have to do to accomplish that?"

Fran Capo
CHICKEN SOUP FOR THE WOMAN'S SOUL

Sometimes knowing how to be in charge is as important as knowing how to let go.

Lizanne Southgate
A SECOND CHICKEN SOUP
FOR THE WOMAN'S SOUL

$\mathcal{I}$'ve learned that my happiness has to come from within.

Laurie Waldron
CHICKEN SOUP FOR THE WOMAN'S SOUL

She believed that if you treated people right, the way you would want to be treated, God would do the rest.

Cindy Hensley McCain
as told to Gina Bridgeman
A SECOND CHICKEN SOUP
for the WOMAN'S SOUL

$\mathcal{M}$y mother taught me that our world is much too large—or too small, take your pick—not to have time to reach out to one another.

Lynn Rogers Petrak
CHICKEN SOUP FOR THE WOMAN'S SOUL

$\mathcal{I}$ love her because she makes more of my world and my life than I can make of them by myself.

Ron C. Eggertsen
A SECOND CHICKEN SOUP
for the WOMAN'S SOUL

$\mathcal{K}$ind words can be short and easy
to speak, but their echoes are truly endless.

— *Mother Teresa*

$\mathcal{I}$'ve learned how to put anything together by seeing the dream in the pieces.

Liah Kraft-Kristiane
CHICKEN SOUP FOR THE WOMAN'S SOUL

"*You*'ll be all right, Mom," said the kindergartner leaving for her first day at school. "I'll be home at noon."

Mary Ann Detzler
CHICKEN SOUP FOR THE WOMAN'S SOUL

Every day I thank God for the small kernel of determination—and the support of my friends—who helped find and free the rainbow during that stormiest of times.

Sharon M. Chamberlain
A SECOND CHICKEN SOUP
FOR THE WOMAN'S SOUL

$\mathcal{L}$ove, wherever it comes from,
always looks the same

Jacqueline Hickey
CHICKEN SOUP FOR THE WOMAN'S SOUL

$\mathcal{Y}$ou are delightful just the way you are. Beauty really does come from within a woman. Believe me.

Joanna Slan
A SECOND CHICKEN SOUP
FOR THE WOMAN'S SOUL

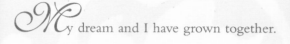

$\mathcal{M}$y dream and I have grown together.

~ *Liah Kraft-Kristaine*
CHICKEN SOUP FOR THE WOMAN'S SOUL

$\mathcal{L}$ife is not always based on the answers we receive, but also on the questions that we ask.

Christy Carter Koski
CHICKEN SOUP FOR THE WOMAN'S SOUL

$\mathcal{T}$o cry is uniquely human, to weep for joy even more so. I cry every day.

Joan Fountain with Carol Kline

CHICKEN SOUP FOR THE WOMAN'S SOUL

Though there were times I would backslide, it was my acceptance of myself in all my strengths and weaknesses that helped me get back up and keep going. My goal was to be better—not perfect.

Joan Fountain with Carol Kline
CHICKEN SOUP FOR THE
WOMAN'S SOUL

It was one of those rare days. You know the kind I mean. When I woke up in the morning, I felt at peace with the world. The sun was shining. The air was crisp with the smell of green. It was a beautiful day, and all was well with the world.

Jean Bole
CHICKEN SOUP
FOR THE WOMAN'S SOUL

$\mathcal{I}$ will laugh when you laugh and cry when you cry. I will remind myself that you are a child, not a grownup, and I will enjoy being your mom.

Diana Loomans
CHICKEN SOUP FOR THE WOMAN'S SOUL

*N*obody has ever measured, not even

poets, how much the heart can hold.

 *Zelda Fitzgerald*

Our scars do matter. They tell us that we have lived, that we haven't hidden from life. When we see our scars plainly, we can find in them...our own unique beauty.

Diana Golden
CHICKEN SOUP FOR THE WOMAN'S SOUL

$\mathcal{W}$e cannot do great things—only small things with great love.

 Mother Teresa

True friends are the ones who never leave your heart, even if they leave your life for a while.

Philip Chard
submitted by Laurie Waldron
CHICKEN SOUP FOR THE
WOMAN'S SOUL

*J*ust saying aloud, "I forgive you,"
changed my whole inner experience from
self-doubt to peacefulness. I let go of
"should have," "could have," and "I wish."
In the process I forgave me, too.

Rosemarie Giessinger
CHICKEN SOUP
FOR THE WOMAN'S SOUL

Spending time with my mom has
taught me the importance of slowing down.
I finally understand the meaning of a term
I've heard a million times: quality time.

David Farrell

CHICKEN SOUP FOR THE WOMAN'S SOUL

*F*ar away there in the sunshine are my highest aspirations. I may not reach them, but I can look up and see their beauty, believe in them, and try to follow them.

Louisa May Alcott

I have always found the strength I needed, but only with God's help.

Charlotte Adelsperger
A SECOND CHICKEN SOUP
FOR THE WOMAN'S SOUL

There is something to be said about leaving a piece of yourself behind in the form of children.

Kay Cordell Whitaker
CHICKEN SOUP FOR THE WOMAN'S SOUL

*O*ut there on the long road of daily living, who knows what will happen? There will be long days filled with sweet monotony. Bright moments of joy. And tedious hours of sorrow. I wish for you the full spectrum of life.

Daniel Schantz
A SECOND CHICKEN SOUP
FOR THE WOMAN'S SOUL

$\mathcal{M}$other taught me to tell the truth....
She taught me the value of working for the
things you want.

~ *Carita Barlow*
as told to Carol McAdoo Rehme
A SECOND CHICKEN SOUP
FOR THE WOMAN'S SOUL

$\mathcal{A}$ true family is not always one's own flesh and blood. It is a climate of the heart.

Shirley Barksdale
A Second Chicken Soup
for the Woman's Soul

$\mathcal{I}$magination is the highest kite
one can fly.

 *Lauren Bacall*

Would you like some tea before you go? At our house, we think of tea as liquid sunshine.

Roberta Messner, R. N., Ph.D.
A SECOND CHICKEN SOUP
for the WOMAN'S SOUL

"Grandma, I've spilled my honey all over your brand new carpet." Grandma Ruby knelt down, looked tenderly in Sheena's tearful eyes and said, "Don't worry, sweetheart, we can get you more honey."

Lynn Robertson
CHICKEN SOUP
FOR THE WOMAN'S SOUL

$\mathcal{D}$on't ever underestimate your dreams in life. Anything can happen if you believe. Not a childish, magical belief. It means hard work, but never doubt that you can do it, with God's help.

Virginia Schantz
as told to Daniel Schantz
A SECOND CHICKEN SOUP
for the WOMAN'S SOUL

As soon as you feel too old to do a thing, do it!

Margaret Deland

$\mathcal{S}$ometimes to get our full attention, God must knock us down, or at least make us blind.

Barbara Jeanne Fisher
A SECOND CHICKEN SOUP
for the WOMAN'S SOUL

$\mathcal{A}$ll of us have a secret self that needs to be encouraged and shared with those we love.

Grazina Smith
CHICKEN SOUP FOR THE WOMAN'S SOUL

$\mathcal{I}$f you stop, you'll never reach

your dream.

Charles Slack
as told by Bessie Pender
CHICKEN SOUP
FOR THE WOMAN'S SOUL

$\mathcal{Y}$ou don't stop laughing
because you grow old;
You grow old
because you stop laughing.

 *Michael Pritchard*

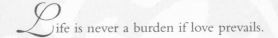

$\mathcal{L}$ife is never a burden if love prevails.

$\mathcal{C}$*harlotte Adelsperger*
A SECOND CHICKEN SOUP
FOR THE WOMAN'S SOUL

*D*eep inside I know where the dream comes from and what it means. It is God's way of reminding me of some unfinished business in my life.

Virginia Schantz
as told to Daniel Schantz
A SECOND CHICKEN SOUP
FOR THE WOMAN'S SOUL

Complete and unconditional forgiveness brought me soul-soothing peace and opened the door to a life I never dreamed possible.

Rosemarie Giessinger
CHICKEN SOUP FOR THE WOMAN'S SOUL

There are high spots in all of our lives, and most of them have come about through encouragement from someone else.
I don't care how great, how famous or successful a man or woman may be, each hungers for applause.

George M. Adams

The cream of enjoyment in this life is always impromptu. The chance walk; the unexpected visit; the unpremeditated journey; the unsought conversation or acquaintance.

 *Fanny Fern*

Giving myself permission to accept the help I needed was the single most important thing I could have done for myself.

Shelley Peterman Schwarz
A SECOND CHICKEN SOUP
FOR THE WOMAN'S SOUL

Don't just count your years, make your years count.

Ernest Meyers

Opportunities are usually disguised by hard work, so most people don't recognize them.

 *Ann Landers*

$\mathcal{T}$here is hope even in the smallest of things.

— *Melody Arnett*
CHICKEN SOUP FOR THE WOMAN'S SOUL

Today a new sun rises for me;
everything lives, everything is animated,
everything seems to speak to me of my
passion, everything invites me to cherish it.

Anne de Lenclos

$\mathcal{I}$ cry for all the years I wanted and needed to cry and didn't. I cry for the loneliness and pain I've felt. I cry for the sheer delight of being alive. I cry for the pleasure that moving my body brings, and for the ability to dance and stretch and sweat. I cry in gratitude.

Joan Fountain
with Carol Kline
CHICKEN SOUP
FOR THE WOMAN'S SOUL

*W*hen asked how she still appears young despite her difficult lifestyle, Mother Teresa replied, "Sometimes a good feeling from inside is worth much more than a beautician."

$\mathcal{W}$holeness has nothing to do with missing parts and everything to do with spirit.

Diana Golden
CHICKEN SOUP FOR THE WOMAN'S SOUL

$\mathcal{I}$n this hustle-bustle world we live in, it's so much easier to charge something on a credit card rather than give a gift of the heart. And gifts of the heart are especially needed.

Sheryl Nicholson
CHICKEN SOUP
FOR THE WOMAN'S SOUL

It was that way with everything: Instead of doing things for me, or excusing me, my mother insisted I find a way to do them myself.

Stacey Nasalroad
CHICKEN SOUP FOR THE WOMAN'S SOUL

$\mathscr{I}$f someone listens, or stretches out a hand, or whispers a kind word of encouragement, or attempts to understand a lonely person, extraordinary things begin to happen.

 *Loretta Girzaitis*

She reminded me that as women, we enjoy a special kind of kinship, even if we're really not all that alike.

Lynn Rogers Petrak
CHICKEN SOUP FOR THE WOMAN'S SOUL

$\mathcal{N}$othing in life is so hard that you

can't make it easier by the way you take it.

 *Ellen Glasgow*

*W*hat is the worst thing that can happen if I don't succeed? The answer is, I simply don't succeed! And what's the best thing that can happen? I succeed! What more can life ask of you: Be yourself and have a good time!

Fran Capo
CHICKEN SOUP
FOR THE WOMAN'S SOUL

$\mathcal{W}$e need romance in our lives;
how we love to get sentimental cards and
love letters.

❦ *Bobbies Lippman*
CHICKEN SOUP FOR THE WOMAN'S SOUL

$\mathcal{G}$od gives us love. Something to love,
he lends us.

$\mathcal{O}$ *Norma R. Larson*
A Second Chicken Soup
for the Woman's Soul

$\mathcal{T}$hings happen inside, and things happen outside, but what's most important is what [a woman] thinks about herself.

Roy Exum
A SECOND CHICKEN SOUP
FOR THE WOMAN'S SOUL

$\mathcal{D}$on't worry—it doesn't matter. You don't have to be like anyone else because you're already perfect. We're all unique, we're all different. And you, too, have something wonderful to share with the world.

Jennifer Read Hawthorne
CHICKEN SOUP FOR THE WOMAN'S SOUL

$\mathcal{T}$he richness of the human experience
would lose something of rewarding joy if
there were no limitations to overcome.

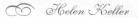 *Helen Keller*

$\mathscr{I}$f there was a problem in the community, [she] just naturally assumed that she was supposed to be part of the solution.

Edgar Bledsoe
CHICKEN SOUP FOR THE WOMAN'S SOUL

I faced the woman in the mirror and asked, "How will you ever know what you can do if you don't try?"

Chris Mullins

A SECOND CHICKEN SOUP
FOR THE WOMAN'S SOUL

$\mathscr{A}$s I see it, no matter how much stuff you buy, no matter how much money you make, you really only get to keep three things in life…. One, your experiences; two, your true friends; and three, what you grow inside yourself.

~ *Philip Chard*
submitted by
Laurie Waldron
CHICKEN SOUP
FOR THE WOMAN'S SOUL

$\mathscr{N}$o one is just an anything. Each of us has gifts and talents. We need not limit ourselves by such small definitions. I know what I can do when I listen to my heart and live from there.

Geery Howe
A SECOND CHICKEN SOUP
FOR THE WOMAN'S SOUL

$\mathcal{I}$n the worst of times, creativity and resourcefulness had given us the best of times.

$\mathcal{S}$heryl $\mathcal{N}$icholson
CHICKEN SOUP FOR THE WOMAN'S SOUL

*L*ove doesn't just sit there like a stone; it has to be made, like bread, remade all the time, made new.

Ursula K. Le Guin

$\mathcal{S}$ometimes we were simply silent,
enjoying each other's companionship and
nothing more; sometimes there was no need
for words.

Veronica Hilton
A SECOND CHICKEN SOUP
FOR THE WOMAN'S SOUL

"*How* do you deal with the overwhelming needs, the disease, the death?" I asked. "You look into one face," she said, her voice filled with peace, "and you continue the work." And know that God will do the rest.

Cindy Hensley McCain
as told to Gina Bridgeman
A SECOND CHICKEN SOUP
FOR THE SOUL

$\mathcal{T}$hose who love deeply never grow old;
they may die of old age, but they
die young.

 — *Benjamin Franklin*

$\mathcal{I}$t has been said that love is not
something you find; it's something you do.

Ron C. Eggertsen
A SECOND CHICKEN SOUP
FOR THE WOMAN'S SOUL

A coincidence is a small miracle

where God chose to remain anonymous.

Heidi Quade

$\mathcal{I}$ looked on child rearing not only as a work of love and duty but as a profession that was fully as interesting and challenging as any honorable profession in the world, and one that demanded the best I could bring to it.

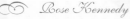 *Rose Kennedy*

$\mathcal{W}$hile both joy and sorrow are fleeting, and often intertwined, love has the power to overcome both. And love can last forever.

Deb Plouse Fulton
A SECOND CHICKEN SOUP
FOR THE WOMAN'S SOUL

$\mathcal{D}$reams are renewable. No matter what our age or condition, there are still untapped possibilities within us and new beauty waiting to be born.

 Dale Turner

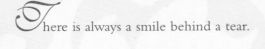

There is always a smile behind a tear.

Helen Luecke
A SECOND CHICKEN SOUP
FOR THE WOMAN'S SOUL